ASSORTED POEMS - 5

OMPRAKASH

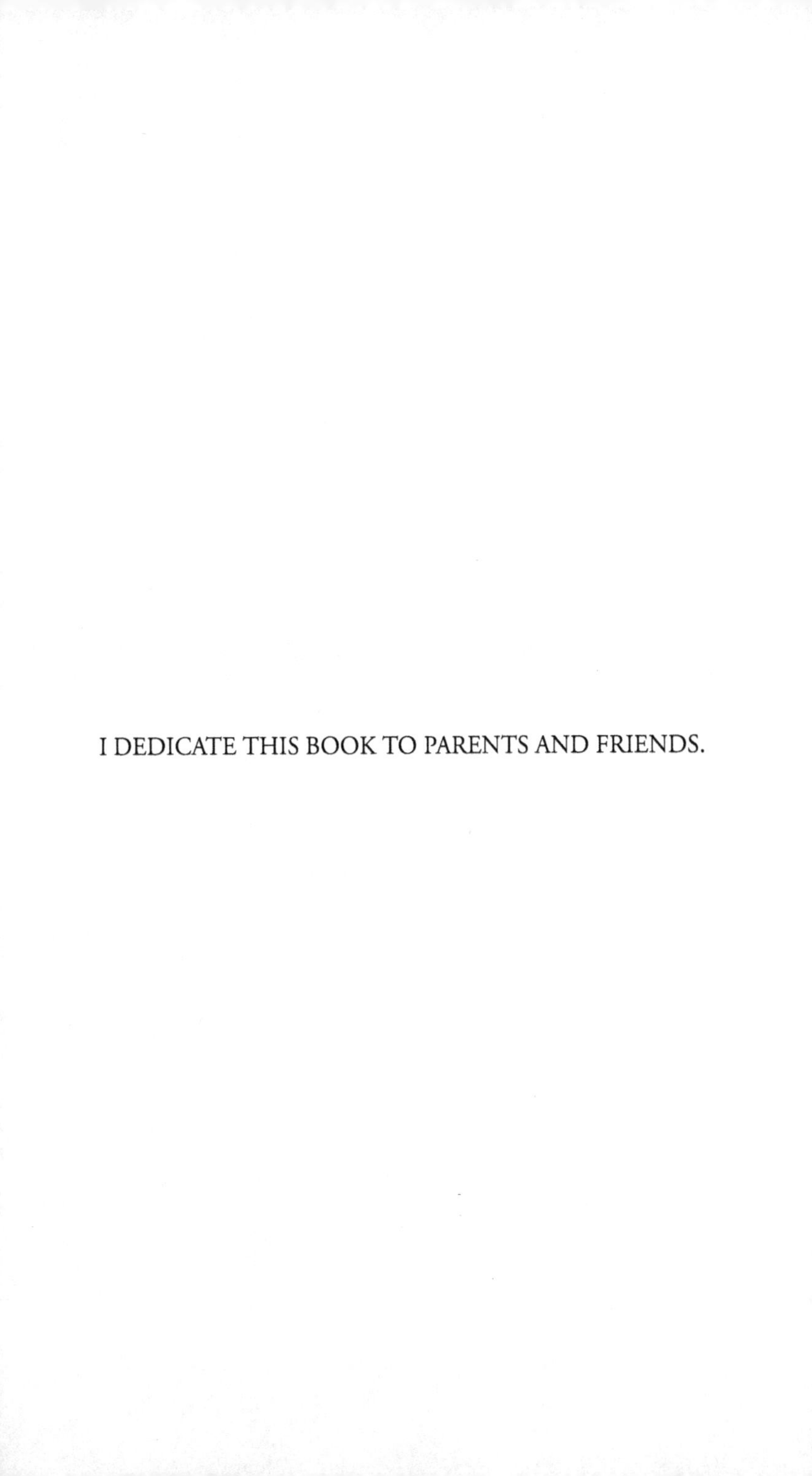

I DEDICATE THIS BOOK TO PARENTS AND FRIENDS.

Contents

Contents

1. God really a worth entity

Believed creator of university,

Relieved self by blesship,

commotion between many creatures a dictatorship,

promotion because to enhance his thoughts,

elation by human never humaneship,

dilation after difficulties not divineship,

he could be sensational because emotionship,

he, author of other-selves so writership,

how he was created so cause us derangeship,

vow to god not to do again same, so mistakeship,

sow our thoughts to reap what-ship,

who is superlative , whether god or 'ship,

shall we compete with god? who-ship and why-ship,

do we have god of god , an unknownship,

yes we have, who is originless, godship,

Godship and worship him is an undefineship,

so us better carry our workship,

which show us what could have been a "?ship"

"?ship" is "i know ship".

so god surely is worthship.

worship him through hymnship!!!

2. Western vers(e,u)s Indian voices

indian cares writership contrary to mine'ship,

"i care my presence " so westernship,

"do you mind by recognizing me", query by western

"did i suppressed you?, why again by indian verses,

many creativity became and become in western,

money never easier for creativity by indian,

honey poured over western verses,

horny pecked toward indian writers;,

western verses born out of nature,

our verses dying due to self-torture,

western lead a ascetic life,

ours lied to.....and hence pleasure life,

western die out of creative writership,

our thoughts never dying,

"because thought not our own,

"God alone claim authorship"

As origin of original thoughts not belongs to us,

only those who do self-denial alone......won't claim mineship,

which western are not ....but indian along from were to where?

3. Philosophy about anything - anyone

"I know ", what i don't know now or later,

earthly to celestial bodies vary identities,

discipline of disciples learnt by themselves,

distant ideas and grapple thoughts,

Gather ideas and grapple thoughts,

gear-up for next vision from where,

clear often naive leads to notion become unclear,

philosophies of myself might become old when new'selves born,

philosophers are always old, but philosophies are older,

nature's philosophies , well understanding,

natural philosophers know how to understand,

so what exactly is philosophy?

just to leave earth peacefully,

will it work? not sure according to philosophically,

so no is philosopher as philosophy is a mist,

because pain of living a philosophical life is a rejoice,

now philosophy exist but can't exist philosophers,

because study of man is also philosophy,

philosophy is an eternal word untold,

philosopher is an short-lived and said....

4. ......identify ....GOD...

lack of appetite, like about god,
alike and aloof once ideas about god,
when starve? food is god,
when thought? no to god,
ask many-selves identifying god about,
mask and let yourselves mood out,
meant for living ; mean to thought weaving,
origin of "god "thought arise when and where?
"virgin about god?"left to individual,
literature , science-scene-creature are temporary,
above could be permanent when never over,
far-above and far-fetched is never thought about god,
fear about life-death , pursue about good god,
why we are living? none got solution,
waist level thought about god,
waste of god literacy, just about his behaviour,
crestfallen won't exist when god won't,
crust of human creature birth is everlasting,
no specific texture about god ,all portraits vary upon how we
are...

5. History an unavoidable science

Birth of science and death of history remain inseparable,
torque between wars measured is science,
when war over it become history,
when grown science become history,
histrionic traits happened due to history,
plutonic character established worthwhile,
caricature between history and science,
care-taken because mystery exists every scene,
peers satisfy appetite , will it is science or become history,
peek of science become history,
meek of history and hence science developed,
"made in country", become history,
hint be history, shall be science,
work hard to become history and science,
history learners rule world,
science preachers rotate world,
thanks to science to create history.

6. Please help me

many thoughts travel all through universe,
money , mate and so on, so cause versus,
honey , horny exchanged between us,
hate mankind, why sixth sense!
might man-kithandkin cursed and so on....
love and food essential for pleasant thought essence,
grown between shy and shy,
frown on account of frustration,
could be blessed and blissful,
mood swing between and because,
doodle about universe, dude "how are you! verse",
fumble between celestial bodies by god,
grumble planets like earth etc.,.
i am tired god , what is remaining,
i am now good, remaining is to do what,
please help many-selves for betterment of universe,
UNIVERSE---(UN)known (I")ntelligent (VERSE),
thank you universe for saving and serving mine....

7. Why i shouldn't

ever since earth born new revolutions came,
boisterous and mysterious came long way,
pompous living not immature since away,
sensual feeling know once freedom,
care taken motherly, cure taken fatherly,
obvious reasoning exist well before,
seen wheedle existence be fear,
shy calamity hence sly dexterity,
she done enough ; he still doing,
birth process, mirth oneself,
becoming godness essential allness,
upcoming noneness could be forthcoming
fauna generally good animosity,
froth comes; betroth happen hapless,
instantaneous infinitesimal aggravate it been,
constant gratitude so converse your attitude,
propose yourselves what i was,
learn from where it can't be,
should or shouldn't , none clear,
god made of should, so us don't know .

8. Journals a good invention

universe exists followed by it behaves as....

universal theory never came and went,

all entities identify one after many-selves

all along we have earthly pleasures,

when i wake , i realize thee and thou,

when yours become ours there are thou,

universe exists for many observations,

coagulate thoughts; inculcate it for new findings,

coax one another exists, where and were,

man record for replication to fellows,

nightmare propel one's thought any direction,

mine invention so follow convention,

night merely solve many dimension,

might GOD; mighty good,

recorded events published as journal,

accord authorship, rarely author,

chord between theories bend what was unbent,

still no one assured birth of many theories,

till we propagate ; until you migrate,

however we record ; unknown probabilities are.

9. Why unnecessarily?

want to work all throughout day,

would ache for creativity as it should have been,

sail throughout earth to explore,

gall because of ,"why due to ?".

some of our activity deactivate ,

son of god-father, sun to be his notion,

sane out of toil, apply yourself soiled,

shun various discipline of earth planet,

shine curious disciple, not necessarily planned,

plot to develop earth , pond fulfilled,

plough earth cause, sought cease,

gloves of activity raised screen,

sleight of hand , dexterity develop men,

slight sluggish enhances to be meant,

unknown of unnecessary is a conjunction,

unnecessary ever a knowledge at any juncture,

proficiency and efficiency about many-selves is definitely unnecessary.

10. Teacher , who taught

"dedication", a synonym for teacher,
abdication never a solution for them,
digestion of thought propagated to us,
astute always not an objective,
"ask yourselves ", been their adjective,
mask not interested for, so we seek,
"invention done every dawn", teaching done,
sanction of habit cause suction of knowledge,
elocution to elation penetrate knowhow,
friction between students and teacher enhance faction,
"restriction of thought ", taught by teacher,
why? because of teacher nature calamity,
good or bad, taught what was thought,
guard ourselves ;from nature

11. Intelligent a curse

how defined or decorated never a standard,

sow seed so to reap wondered,

moo to vow whatever thought,

goose selectively see through though,

mouse dictate science and technology,

however we restrict thought it erupt,

neither ...either none is fool,

better get along ; litter recycled,

slag and lag .....what are they,

even we don't think what to thought,

heaven and its ally cause seven,

thoughts always never curse,

texture of human body; bless or curse,

trait define after many definition,

theology and theory vary hence new version,

medicine of earth come up with new math-culture,

how one thought ? still death not prevented,

solution: not in our hand when we weep.

12. Music composed due to......

god blessed space with planets and stars,

good thought caused so many steer,

guard against humanity exist due to music,

ghostly existence enhance peevishness,

ghastly appearance soothed due to music,

mostly mused for new developments and etc.,.

fast and feast support envelopments are,

mince such that hence caused hare,

hence suction often; finger movements mechanized ,

since earthly developments produce hearth,

sine and cosine waves exists for vibration,

sin and win situation recorded inertly,

devastation too described with music,

origin of never known until we,

predicted pronounce of coined phrases also,

fabricated god and music hand in hand,

music valley all across the space,

notes are recorded and hence nodes spawn,

neat sound and hence wheat grinding,

weed and seed separated also music,

any sound waves interpreted music,

god and mood; described and interpreted,

large or lounge music enhances mood,
(M)ate (U)niversal (S)c(I)ence (C)reativity.

13. Paperwork a best practice

earth has many probabilities into,

worth can measured as which out,

scarcity exists due to lack of records,

tenacity firm; dew only after seclusion,

firmness form when followed by recluse,

facts were not recorded as such ,

fix where happened and so what happened,

octogenarian of senility classify towards,

many generations happened and but cultivated none,

moon to sun many theories exist to glow,

man often classify this remaining,

when records are realised revolution faster,

woods destroyed and architecture born,

would be done from dusk to dawn,

still to think are more so often,

heated exchange of words recorded,

feat achieved cause new accord,

seat fastened to scene by science,

freek hastened either or bother,

geek towards rupture cause boisterous,

meek only solution for us either,

eloquence of one's potential happen,

frequency of achievement happen due to,

14. Life and death- an un'definable nature

unthinkable ,unremain inconclusive forever,

uncountable species and so non-explorable,

cast as undefined behaviour because unthinkable,

none-we as shall and will untraceable,

unknown of many assume to be known,

philosophy thought as undeclared,

study of unthinkable becomely unduly unrespectable,

umbrage unaffected other of self,

unctuous mankind not necessarily un',

ask yourself , why unnecessary so,

astounding belief we can't study nature,

postpone , procrastinate , not doing whether favour or are,

i unremain conclusive as life and death not exist,

centuries went still nature undictatable by us,

LIFE - (L)onely (I)ntelligence about (FE)ar

DEATH - (D)irect to h(EA)r(TH),

15. Abode and Abide

ever since earth born we abide and abate,

though we thought our motto extinguish,

through our nature we became part of languish,

nowadays , oath hath comes near buy by,

vow to ourselves to sow good seed,

very much essential and so essence of greed,

however abode not forever as such thinks,

oust by cow and so sun never sets,

most of siblings live like get-together,

father and counterpart make go-getter,

tether knots with nature because otherwise,

whether got by self-sacrifice been wise,

sloth and loathe subside our notion,

froth of thoughts reed of mention,

betrothal happen haplessly, so cause pride,

Cbehemoth slay one among ourselves breed,

wear mask to prevent ourselves identify,

mere musk too advent myself addendum,

more to ask for meant and hence,

preemptive living enforce imperative task,

weaving one's culture remains unweaved,

sheaves of paper cause sleeves of undulyness,

abode and abide cause hatred if united,

they must coagulate or else not to promulgate...

16. Constitutional instigate

where to bygone such that obscene untoward,

were self- bigotry hence freelancing,

are there any satisfaction promulgate,

are they many artistic coagulate,

about disciple prevaricate much more,

abate discuss public meant mere,

articulate divest unfortunate satisfactory,

gesticulate disrupt behaviour obfuscate activity,

mend potion; mad occur sideways ,

amend whatever described about eruption,

gamut evolve so as to abet fabrication,

eloped from profession with instigation,

galloped form confession which mincing

followed-up causes unnecessary meaning,

gallons of thoughts settled once again,

alone ceases to exist; animals became and again,

a lawn cleanse fist when cleaned agog,

absolve done every dawn so better smog,

obscene doing very often soon hotter fog,

clean habit every preposterous mist.

17. Diplomacy, a horn

envy bring human greed over other's seed,
awry of emotions due to fluctuate weed,
seen maim and crippled activity,
weep set aside in favour of whom?
texture over conjecture eject emotion,
mixture of events promote denotation,
what to do? goodness kept and wept,
vote thoughts; nice and wise,
vault kept inside once commotion seize,
salt and sugar thought after siesta,
fault happened due to killing an d eaten,
more often than not very much,
mere conjecture about living won't,
mare of nightmare seduce one's....
mother alone been in spite of above.
bother loneliness being, despite often one down,
nest living won't teach what towards,
away weave your thoughts how agony,
neigh a stallion and cast of a agony,
mate of mighty, sight seen caution,
most of us now cunning notion,
must caste prevaricate aloof dawn,
private thought propagate none harm,

diplomacy cost lack of transparency,
affluence caste luck for diplomat.

18. Thought-killing human, if so how to prevent it ?!

where is origin of thoughts? i k(no)w,
were it could have been because of now,
wear knowledge; to declare "i know",
calm down every dawn to become non-moon,
call yourself to ask, " why, what, how....";
cage followed to skyscrapers after civilizations,
sage become mine , so thoughts immature,
saintly living declare, " i own what.....i disown",
ages i was loquacious declare i know(some, none, any)thing,
fuse this process to extinguish thoughts forever,
fist impact causes us to cease the competitions,
mist created by man, must we win other man,
gist of above s, " thought(s) seduce oneself",
history to geography proclaim we grown,
kno-(one)w claim thoughts can be arrested,
knell rings all over our environment,
sail all over the place, time is unavoidable,
gall and annoy impact leads to enrichment,
love yourself, but will it stop the thoughts,
lawn to something, law to be broken,

flown place to place; glow slow exists,

inventions and discoveries what are those,

man thoughts what has to be why though?

mane exists for human which due to BRAIN,

"(B)ecause (R)ationalize (A)gainst (IN)tellectual" of many-
self,

i hate thoughts why?become and became,

thoughts are fools and fouls to become.....

19. Wavelength of god

seen after and after of imperative,
be whatever happened through thoughts,
because mind controllably uncontrollable,
cause and because due to sluggishness,
hard to perceive; but no way to conceive,
shard projections inside body nowhere,
protrude from earth and still more to go,
attitude came long way so no seclude,
attire wear upon ;satire come nowhere,
atheism exists forlorn hence no lone,
monotonous thought propagate preclude,
agony perspire leads to mahogany aspire,
agape on instances; elope with goddess,
agog much to seen, fervour all known never,
festive season; worship to offer none noun,
aesthetic and ascetic side by side,
clemency causes euphoria followed by elasticity,
caricature thoughts analyse agony towards,
cacophony nemesis towards god; none impact,
malicious events causes avarice all alone,
benevolence and malevolence exists across,
nostalgia goddess when from heaven,
navigate god but ends in nowhere

frustrate followed by feast begin and end,

gourmet an identity whatsoever,

scripture by man made, made him hymn,

prevalent thought through sand and rock,

quiet and chant sandwiched,

rationalize god to become human fraction,

raucous , sensible , calm exists wherever,

lot of sensible noun-sense said about divine,

only those who remain now "i unknown " become....

20. Made of what

physical perception cause whom to be grown,
metaphysical quantum erases abundance,
virtual leap exist among men and alliance,
value elope with; as mind travels,
void agape seduce earthly and heavenly gravel,
with mental and physical renewable,
wheat causes white mess to become illegible,
thoughts beginning fluctuate drastic ones' wellness,
triumph and trivial is solution unsolved,
tree and so free waves part of nature,
surrounding probability can be unnature,
can't deny; only to accept as it is creature,
incantation worthwhile segment and,
invincible none permanency; neither short-lived,
gone can be dusk; alone dawn forthcoming.
gawk fluctuation after many thoughts soaked,
plenty and saintly living enrich,
awry reinvent and reincarnation,
later replication also done envision,
mate between thoughts so new vision,
might gather toward celestial collision,
meander waves of cosmology mention,
flamboyance across thoughts eradicate denotation,

so far none sure as such;

confusion followed by crystal clear solution,

elation happens which to hapless,

none, none! we are made of what ?!;

complete this unknowingly partial....

21. Truth about life

life uncommonly miracle, rarely oracle,
list of things thinking during the sick,
care taken occurs at worse during,
cure abduction recur waste enduring,
liquid proposal ; worthwhile objective,
liquidate appraisal dearth all-over subjective,
inspiration occur after series often,
perspiration after endurance and so sequence,
aspiration caused frequently,
mainly due to maim approaches adequately,
language so often deranged ; why?
languid followed by lagoon of knowledge,
siesta become meaningless;
feast approaches to mutilate,
aghast due to failure of philosophy;
agony lesson and followed by treason;
god realization happen because hapless.

22. God in translated form

religions exist; but differences deny so often,
relegate future predictions as him many deducted,
hymn repetition , him care-take benevolence,
maim due to violence and so often malevolence,
poignancy about godliness educate unknown,
magnanimous living followed by dexterity kill oneself,
animosity between god noneness,
adversity among human cause none humane,
effective dwelling saturate unknown digging,
effigy followed diligent work progress godliness birth,
perspiration during thought process is adjective,
aspiration achieved but noneness emptied,
lone thinkers at last have lawn of thoughts.

23. why to ???

imperative !? gave lot of breakthrough,

when undecided by individual ; hence and thence,

commence knowledge about theory preceded by pragmatic,

once came the solution, accepted by mob,

less thought gave birth? followed by infiniti'sm

loss of frustration, followed by many productivism,

laws and lettuce go hand in hand,

lawn preparation , gone many perspiration,

gone piracy , adopted quack,

why so?? remain known after unknown

who etc frustum , only peer thoughts,

whom and followed by boon through,

mean living effervescence and when settled ; nice fragrance,

god is unavoidable discussion with no conclusion,

so WHY is predictably soon....

24. Astrology and astute

god and going goodness is obfuscate,

goad about cling to the society confiscate,

clever presumption leads victorious,

leverage once thought about vicious,

lives and life about society hence,

calves worry about their unknown,

leaves worshiped by god though,

lotion prepared out of greens,

potion given to rectify some wound during portion,

preparation either leads astro-thought,

debate between astrology and astute(astronomy),

duty bait and saint obey astro'-,

primogeniture and pristine discuss about the randomness in god,

fracture in astrology leads to astuteness,

meander a worthwhile seclusion after solution,

arraign about phenomenon would and worth,

sovereign abet celestial bodies give astute birth,

astrology define one's astute syllogism ,

happen vice-versa when astute defined through undefined behaviour.

25. Literacy a gamble

celestial bodies education a worthwhile,

colloquial language is an impromptu,

eloquence achieved after serious of frustration,

affluent happen after hapless confrontation,

mother educate, other obfuscate about,

man made calculate either what sprout,

moon and ; mourn about it cares,

measles gave knowledge about human form,

meander gather and together from,

molecules knowledge what is nomenclature,

....all along and so far illiterate,

when shared boundlessly we shiver,

whence and hence happen parallely,

mute the knowledge to fellow would propagate he hadn't,

clear vision after series of serious,

clever vice rafter once thought through,

cluster of been and beings and hence effervescence of nature,

lacklustre during knowledge gather suture,

waste of time till waist tired creature,

worst thing is yet to come so better calm....